MW00442362

malepoet.

Original Cover Art provided by Gnashing Teeth Publishing.

The font used is Malgun Gothic.

The cover font is Elephant Pro.

Editor-in-Chief Karen Cline-Tardiff

Assistant Editor Jennifer Taylor

Printed in the United States of America

ISBN 978-1-7340495-6-5

Non-Fiction: Poetry

Non-Fiction: Poetry – LGBT

Thank you, LINDA

welcome to
Placitas / ABQ!

malepoet.

PW Covington

PLACITAS / NM

May 2023

Panoply

Sometimes I look back on these decades of living oddly and try to understand. Sometimes I try to weigh the cost. Things won, things lost, and I feel like there are dreams still out there but I really like staying home now. Sometimes, I slow down. I catch the stench of hair on fire. Stoplights and city limit land mines. And what about ol' PW out there somewhere On the Road scribbling wildly into that leather journal some lover gave him? Sleeping it off in a motel somewhere south of Dallas? Smoking cigarettes in the rain beside the Mississippi behind that beignet place? Ordering off the Value Menu at Wendy's in Terre Haute? Neck-deep in some Chuck Taylor manuscript? Plummeting into his 50's, lost tonight, still looking for a home to leave?

Played out like some freakshow calliope tune upstaged by poetry slam hip-hop globetrotters? Hiding redemption at all costs. It's in the comings and goings and the in-between places, that I have always stood. Down the barrels of cannons and derringers I've danced with blessed dark wonder. If you want to stay with me forever you can stay forever or only until the moon disappears and all the truck stop supernovas turn to catastrophe. We could smoke out and we could make love together or it could all fall out of sight. Either way we are all perfectly as we should be. It's not so much that I don't believe there is a God. It's more like I'm not truly convinced that, if He does exist, that He is on our side, at all.

Looking for the Last Great American Whale

I spent a June day sitting on a California
beach
Where cauliflower fields give way to sandy
dunes

I smoked and sat and stared with Biff Loman
eyes past
The rolling, green turquoise, surf
I was hoping to catch a glimpse of
Some
 last, great, American, whale
Through the haze blown in from the ocean
Sea foam glowing iridescent in the native
afternoon

The pale sun burned through fog low clouds
for only minutes at a time

The crisp winds would be called winter cold

in Texas

A half continent away

Behind me

I watched sea dragon seaweed masses

Pushed in by the waves

And found bleached crab carapaces on sand

But, I did not see

Any Lou Reed

Underground

Great American

Whales

That day

Green Mill

Broadway snow and slush in April
Parking meters take a breather
And let us keep the change
Until next morning, Monday

Dark space
Deep place
"Cash only" hand written by the door
Poetry tonight
As it has been
    and will be

Come in from the wet snow
Slam the door

Turn table jukebox. 78's
"Lydia, oh, Lydia
    Have you met Lydia?"

The wooden bar wraps around the room

It's Pabst on draft tonight
5 bucks a pint
I'm tryin' to save my cash
Still drinking on Sioux Falls' haul
Saving up for a down payment on a new
Second-hand soul
No longer needed
By some transplant, who's left for California
When I step on stage
A pilgrim
Of the word and world and the void
And of Broadway and passion and of, of, of
Truthiness-ish communion
With Palm Unit rhythm section
Bass, piano, and drums

Jazz and strong drink tabernacle
Rooms just like this

In April

Equal in glorious, dark, obscurity
Here for the words

When Wine Keeps Time
(the fucking)

I've been paid for poetry
In glances
In smiles of co-conspirators downtown
In truck stop coffee, diner grits and biscuits
In bumps of coke and tokes out by the
    stairs

In the attention of women and college boys
The twinkie ones
That tongue my asshole like sacred flesh
The middle aged, married, school teachers
    and writerly companions
That have taken my load across their holy
Sephora faces

All that road-sex fucking ever was, was
    fucking

And the fucking rolled like ink across the
    page
Across the page and into canyons
Canyons of the wonderful and terrible at
    night with no regrets

Yet, the fucking has never filled or fulfilled
    me
Like the way your eyes shine
When words are our air
    and only wine
        keeps time

Blue Moon
(The Scene of the Crime)

Return to the scene of the crime

Scoring smoke in nickels and dimes

Rolling on eggshells

From west of the line

Avoid blue light, blue moon

Bumps and grinds

Seek out soup kitchens

Guitar pickin'

And fried chicken

Love lines

Lines should not define

The poetry you find

 Inside

Metaphysical cast-asides

Castaways

   the end of days

Return to the scene of the crime

La crimen

La crimen ferpecto

Say it ain't so

I'm just laying low

Hiding from blonde hair

Blue eyes

    and the goddamned Cotton Eyed Joe

What's the difference?

Between yours and mine...

Put the difference on my visa

Stamp it crooked

Sideways

Like the Tower of Pisa

Like that hemisphere spire

In San Antonio

White tablecloths

And 100-dollar vino

Spin motherfucker

Spin motherfucker

Spin

As blood moons

Blue moons

Super moons

    shine

Return to the scene of the crime

Southern Billboards

I am being screamed at by billboards
Flashing by at 75 miles an hour

Come to our Cowboy Church
Our rock and roll, guitar church
Our biker church
Our church
    our church

God damn

Visit the visitor center
The Indian Mounds
Invest this year in a new time-share
Urgent care, next exit
Free in-room coffee, High Speed Wi-Fi
We'll get you out of your time-share
Spend the night, tonight, in San Augustine

Vasectomy

The billboards on the highway teach me
Abortion stops a beating heart
And that God listens to Christian radio
That winners play the Power Ball Lottery
That lasers can reverse my vasectomy
That the café, just 10 miles up I-75
Has totally bare waitresses, raw steaks
    and clean showers

The billboards in Louisiana argue over
Whose caged tiger lived the longest
Pecan pralines and cracklin's up ahead
Shipyards and refineries are hiring
Mesothelioma lawyers want to hear from
    you
8 nonstops a day from Dairy Queen to the
    West Coast

Click it or ticket

You pick it, you pull it

DWI, just don't do it

Drivers eat free at Exit 173

(And more pralines)

Fried chicken and highway diesel

Vote, vote, vote for this guy

Look how clean his family is

And the stripes on that damned flag

We support our troops and first responders

Do not pick up hitchhikers, prison area

Join us Sunday at our Progressive Church

Hobby Airport

South Houston

Hobby airport

Off one end of

Telephone Road

This is Rodney Crowell country

Stopping here

To switch planes

To switch from coffee to Bourbon

To switch from Bukowski to Burroughs

To consider

Would I rather be taken for

A poser or a cliché?

Black jacket

Middle age

Airport bar asshole

Reading paperback poetry

In public places

The nerve

Hitting the sauce

Every fucking molecule,

Exactly what it looks like

Another actual

Old

White

Writer

Guy

On my way to

Another weekend writers conference

Poser and cliché

Like Bukowski and Burroughs

Waiting on a flight

The fuck outta

Here

El Cajon

The Sonoran Desert and sand dunes
It took that fucking Interstate 8
All day drive from Tucson
To burn the concrete image of my Father
from myself...

Mother dead, 6 months, now
For the better, with all the redecorating

The man now has a back-lit
John Wayne
    cardboard cut-out
Standing in his living room
And a 25 foot tall flag pole
Rising from his tiny
    Texas
        trailer park
           front yard

I do not know him, any more
My father would have once had
   ...I dunno...
      Maybe Captain Kirk...
       Maybe Marilyn Monroe
Do they make cardboard cut-outs of Brian
Wilson?

He gave me science fiction, as a boy
Star Wars
And, Bill Murray in Stripes; taught me how
   to play chess
I followed him into the Air Force,
Then he sent me to prison,
to find my own way

He is still in Texas and I do not miss him
   tonight

I miss you, though

John Prine sings

"It's Gonna be a Long Monday"

And, here I sit

At an Econolodge

In El Cajon

Beside the 8 Interstate

And, I'm smoking Blue Dream

Lonesome in a way

That Wi-Fi pornography can't fix

(Not even the good, amateur, stuff)

Without you

Wishing you could be
    in California with me

The Coldest Place I've Been

The coldest place I've been
Is this over-heated room
Santa Fe trails lead in circles
7 cycles of the Sangre de Christos
I feel I'll always be a visitor, here

Port cities and border towns embrace you
When you show up
With empty pockets and wide eyes
Shaking knees and a mixed-breed,
Free-verse, smile
Treat you like you belong there,
If only for a while

But, this place rips your spleen from your
    side
And goes about its Thursday afternoon

It's the feeling that
The Universe is laughing behind
Your back
At a joke told in a language you've never
worked with
And while everyone
Says they yearn for freedom and something
   new
Very few
Stand prepared to welcome a traveler
Or cast off the familiar

Everyone should be a part of somewhere
They say
But not you
Not me
The coldest place I've been
Is this over-heated room

I'll drink my delusions over ice
Tonight

I'll rise in the morning

And drive west all day

Night time highway navigation

Brings back friendly faces and echoes of
    places

That have held out welcome

Rattle around in roadside men's rooms.

Condom machines and gasoline

Still paying for the gas...

It never lasts long

The eternity of an insular scene

With local heroes, honored through decades

Klatches and cliques

Never approve

Of the language I use

New-In-Town blues

Cold rooms and sad tunes

It never lasts long

Only the Truly Great Poets Ever Die

Only truly great poets ever die
Those whose words, so sharp
They split reality at its core
Sliced every eviscerated emotion
Out of conditioned existence

Most poets live forever
Words compelled to wander, unread, eternal
Hungry ghost manuscripts
Spectral poems, once published,
Forever ignored
Still swimming in the sea of language
Our letters dropped, postage paid
Addressed to particularly no one,
Those, most, that live forever

Only the truly great poets ever die
Ever gain the Nirvana of total rest

The permanence of absence

Their truth so coarse and dense

That it collapses upon itself

Taking the great poet with it

A product of poetic fusion

The remains of the truly great poet

Are nothing at all

    like anything

        most of us lesser equals and

          wandering souls

Would ever call

        poetry

Before Big-Pharma

Look to the corners of the cage
The spaces between stacked sticks of pining
Curing

Look that stash right in the eye
With dynamite glow
Down Miracle Road in Decaturville
And Texarkana never tastes the same

Shut down all those alibis, aligning
And learn the sacred freedom
Of the blame

1987 won't return
Until we learn
To look into the corners of the cage

Regret and cowardice remarketed as virtue
You were all born more evolved than I

Why then, your generational anxiety?
Your crushing self-doubt
And anathema fatalism

Rearview mirrors are only there for safety
They're not designed for navigation
Paralysis is not the same as patience

So what, then, if I end up the last
Chain smoking, dope shooting, shop lifting
Asshole tragic troubadour at the truck stop?

What then, If I end up steering the last
V8 – 5 speed, red rag-top,
Detroit gasoline machine
Down the
Last open Interstate to be found?

What if I am the last one lurking
In your safe space
That can roll a decent joint

Or kiss you in the way
You've never been
Honest enough to admit
That you know you truly need
To be kissed?

Will there be a warning label
Will there be a trigger warning
3 steps ahead of me, at all times?

I already have an attorney on retainer

All your fears and fantasies
Like Percocet and Benzedrine
Get flushed down motel toilets
In the corners

You asked to see what life was like
Before Big-Pharma

Merced

Cardboard bulkhead hotel
    ...motel
Motel 6 in Merced
Second story
And, how I wish
It was the throes of
Illicit lovers
Or a drug-fueled
Libertine orgy
Crashing into my transient, one-night, garret

And not
The tourist -rate seismic reality
Of what sounds like
    dozens of
        tumbling toddlers
From the other side of the wall

As I drink cheap, white, wine
And finally give up on trying to masturbate

Make love, not kids, I say
If you plan on staying
    at the same shit-hole joints
        that I do
           out on the road
           to sleep

My Smile

I keep
A smile
Stashed away
Like a burrowing owl
For infants
At airports
    or in check-out lines
        at retail stores

A goofy
Toothy
Happy, wide-eyed
Thing
Usually kept out of sight
At least
    in sober
        daylight

Rider

Death is my designated driver
Bareback
Home from the Earthly cantina
Of sorrows and indulgence
Down dark alleys and side streets
We avoid the well-lit roads

Until we can't

Clasping at the driver's back
No terror nor trepidation
Past locked and bolted parlor doors
Windows lit by dim and fading lamps
Pale horse hooves on border town
    cobblestones

We all cross that line

Too long down sidewalks too clean to be
Anything but dreams called faith
We reach our limits
And have nowhere to go besides over
I am not holding the reins

I never have

Terrified of testing all that
Individually discovered truth
And atmospherically absorbed experience
When the time arrives
To leave the shadows

The Weight of the Thing

It is the weight of the thing
The dark, deadly, machined
Final and explosive
Sole, undeniable
Weight

In the palm of my hand
The power and wrath it lends me
To pump vengeance into those I deem
    deserving
Or to cancel my own inadequacies
A place to hold onto hope
To control both
For as long as I can
The weight

Of believing that my bets can all be covered
With the right talents

With the right technology
With enough skill
With a full load
Cocked

With fury and failure
In the chamber
Stoned, alone,
In bed
I am fascinated by
The weight of the thing
In the palm of my hand

Indica on the Forenoon Watch

Vague

Undefined

Formless

Not here

Yet,

Not absent

The calm of your face

Three minutes

Before

Sublimation

Like high desert snow

Intoxication

Ego drifts away

On Indica smoke

Cloudy

We

Dissolve into each other

Feeding into traffic

From the entrance ramp

Drifting downstream

With salt and silt

And a thousand dry-land

Wishes, beyond means

Murky

Nebulous

Smoke

Dream

We

Become more

By being

Less

Our Lady of the Snows

So,
I went there
To that shrine at
The Mississippi and Missouri
To Our Lady of the Snows
To catch, perhaps
A flake or two of Rome

Or, the sweet aboriginal aroma
Of roses, abloom, in Guadalupe winter

And, I knelt in silent hope
I even lit a votive
Then, I sat in silence
And, I sat

Stand-up, zero-turn, lawn mowers
Kept it all golf course perfect

Conference center clean

When I left that place
There, below that river bluff
As I turned out, back, upon
The state highway, below
I saw

Clap board brothels lined up
Hawking
Oriental Massage
And St. Clair County's
Largest Gentleman's Club
Three limousines, blocking the entrance
Like some stone at some tomb
Or something, somewhere

And, I understood
Why God
Stopped climbing stairs and seeking out
Such high and pristine places

And came to prefer leaving

Such high and pristine people

Alone

My God

My God
Is that drop dead gorgeous kid
That you never noticed
In front of you
In the line
Outside the club
That the door guy
Lets in
Then
At the last minute
Turns to you and your friend
And says
"Oh, they're with me, too- no cover charge."

Then, once you're in
You never see again

Religion _____?

So,
I'll just believe
    and behave
As I please, and

I'm cool with any church
That wants to claim me

After Jack Kerouac

God is Pooh Bear

God is smoking cigarettes in the calico
  alleyway beside Lucky Dog Books

God is riding the triple 7 bus up

Central Avenue

God is flowing down your thigh after sex

God is unexpected, unintended, and
  unearned glory perfect happenstance

God is a magic gas pump credit card

God is a cop with better things to do

God is you

God is pigeons in Alamo Plaza

God is sleeping in a doorway on Shattuck

God is accordion in a border town cantina

God is working a double shift washing
  dishes at Denny's

God is a light and a free toke of smoke

God is a night without any debt

God is a copy of Leaves of Grass found on a
    park bench

God is cheering in Spanish from the
    right field bleachers at Wrigley

God is popping your back in 5 places

God is the first daffodil of Spring

God is Colorado

God is queer and seeking asylum

God is worn carpet in forest green checks

God is poetry, read at the zoo

God is you

God is God is alive in all we do

God is you, there

God is Pooh Bear

I Know

I'm one little man
    on a bed
In one little room
    of one little place
Down a little dirt alley
    off a little-traveled street
In an oft-forgotten city,
    as cities go

But, I know
The poems of humming birds
And all the mountain trails
To ephemeral
    paradise

Down

Down that muddy bayou

Down

Down those jet planes landing

Down

Telephone Road and Methadone

Down

Down, boy, Down

What has the World Series done for you?

Down

Propped up

Beat Down

Tear the pennant

Down

Kneel

Down

Down that mystery highway

To New Orleans voodoo

Down

Down, women of the world

Down

Down to DuPont Circle

Down to this

Down to Earth

Down, Down, Down

Like Thelonious Monk

Get Down

Down on the skins

Get Down

To get in

Down in Sin

Then up again

Down

Down

The Tristan Chord

Another lost journal
Another lost year
Another lost love
Another lost chance
    another night ends
    another street over
    another tide turns
    another road rises
    another bed burns

Another voice silenced

Another flash
Another shield
Another streak across galactic solitude of
    glory
Collapsed upon itself, melodically

Like Wagner's
Tristan chord
Over
 but not yet finished
 not yet fulfilled
Yearning for yellow daffodils
 from a cold mountain crimson sky at
 dawn
Halcyon

And water bongs
Rights and wrongs and
Mobile homes
Vagabonds and vagrants
Taxi meter dialectics

F# major in the 7th degree
Sun tanned
Beer cans
Buried on a beach

Zero Tolerance

I have zero tolerance for zero tolerance
Second chances should come
With second chances
We need to change climate change
Any line on any map should end
    or run on forever, to make a circle
Stand outside of circles

Free the poets from their classrooms
From the bookshops and coffee houses
Send them to the front lines
Backwaters and grimy places
Fuck clichés into the predawn hours
Roast East Coast editors with French toast
    for breakfast

Oil rigs and ocelots in Texas
Burning...Turn it off! Turn it off!

19th century social family values

Warp our Colonial DNA

Evolve beyond gunboats and mythology

Revolve and see from the outside

Lightning on a summer night

South of Raton Pass

Prohibit prohibition

Choice is what we're selling

Hate is what we're smelling

Why did we stop bombing Fascists?

What is worth dying for?

Life is life is life

    and night is night is night

Multiple Re-Entry

The greatest
Customs and Immigration officers
I ever saw
Stood guard
Atop the bluffs
At Belinda Beach

Salt cedars, twisted
    redwood sentinels
        and eucalyptus
(immigrants, on the shore, themselves)

Roots and branches
Wood and leaves
Bring you back to things terrestrial
For half a mile after that
Grey-washed, rocky cove

They inspect your senses with aromatic
    late spring, welcome
And, slowly, as you declare yourself
With destinations of concrete and real estate
The ocean's never ending,
Lunar tune grows muffled

Here, at this landing
On this shore
At this organic checkpoint of the soul,
These green-clad,
    towering,
        ancient agents
Stamp every sun-blessed, fortune-kissed,
trans-Pacific
Pilgrim's heart that passes
    as
        'multiple re-entry'

The Age of Thunder Lizards

The age of thunder lizards is over
Let songbirds take the air
Liars in Chief don't apologize on the border
To soldiers banking on his yields
Let the frontier guards build their walls
Let the poets tear them down
Let the blood moon rise
    and eclipse itself
With a twangy, country, sound

I'm alright; like the rest of us
Just a little stoned
And I'm okay on the right side
On the outside
Left behind
And, you're okay
You've never believed

If time won't tell, the weather will
Whether this lust will last
However this bust is cast

Would you rather be
Colonized or conquered
Absorbed or assimilated
Watered down or drowned
Served as soup or over rice?

The highway exits roll back upon themselves
Like the House of Eternal Return tends to do
Turning lanes and toll booths
Can go fuck the Catechism
As early morning greyness ensues

Liars in Chief cannot last forever
Reptile kinky sex can show us something
deeper
And coffee waits in heaven on the dash

Cosas y Conceptos

There's that little park
   on Adams Street in Brownsville
With the fountain and the benches
Flanked by border-hopping
Taxi stands, dive bars
   and tiendas full of ropa usada
Matamoros three blocks away

A river
A wall
   and men with guns, still
Tired and peeling, like layers of white plaster
   flaking off
Colonizing brick
I am shedding something here
That I no longer need
I am still
Declaring myself at the border

Refugees and vagabonds, always arriving
Declaring customs at the line

Cosas y conceptos that cannot
Be clearly seen from fogged up tour bus
    windows

I remember when army barracks became
    school rooms
Cavalry stalls made lecture halls
Seeds of progress fertilized by dreams and
    blood and deeds
When walls were repurposed as pedestals
Lifting lonely voices higher
    and freedoms danced upon acordeón
    winds, unbound

The Enemy

The C-130's
Over my mountain garden
Take me back

Sometimes we landed at their airports
Turboprop drone
ZZZauggh!
Or, we'd come in on big, grey, airplanes
Jet engines whining

Or, we landed on silent silk

Sometimes rotor blades
Chopped their air
Like Satan's own mother
Bleating in dark and deadly passionate rage
And they'd hide

Doing their best to dodge and outlast

The hate and ignorance

We carried with us

Strapped to our chests

Slung under our wings

Where cold hearts beat

With the courage of armed 19 year-olds

The bravest of them

Stood up, shot back

Did what they could do

And we were told to

    call them

The enemy

Notre Dame is Burning (4/15/2019)

Notre Dame is burning today, and I am
  driving
Leaving Chicago, again
After mid-April snow
Always driving
Driven on, as if any of this world
Will last forever
Driving fast
Because nothing ever does
Even holy shrines in ancient cities
Ignite and drift away
Cinders and ash, to cinders and ash
From truck stops to gas
Headlong, through corn fields
Chasing down all the catechism
Of combustion

Only our gargoyles survive infernos

This is the week that

They say that

Christ

    Descended

       Into

          Hell

The House of Bourbon

The House of Bourbon would know nothing
Nothing of New Orleans
Or bottles of maguey cactus fantasia fueled
        unicorn nights of whimsy
Yarns exchanged in dressing rooms
Strip-club buttercups

Decadence served from leaky paper plate
        pinwheels
Lost to time and dreams
Chronology unleashed
Like a strangely single shoe left on a By-
Water street
Next to two empty cherry soda cans
Alone

Vacuous sunrises shine
Like dark nopal eyes

And the river smells of streetcar lines at dawn

A Butt (Plug) of Advice

If you've got a butt plug up your ass
When you hit the pipe
    ...that strong-ass sativa,
        something like Jack Herer or
            Green Crack

And you start coughing like
Some old West whorehouse pianoplayer,
All ate up with consumption?

You should probably be sitting down, cat...

Some Exquisite Lingerie

I'd come over
And take a seat on the sofa
With your husband

You'd sit across the room
In that leather, high-back, chair
And pack a bowl

You'd tell me to pull out
My already swelling cock

Then tell him to get down
On the floor before me

Then, after
After he came back
From brushing his teeth

He'd hand me his AmEx
And say that he'd have brunch ready
When we returned, the next day

It only lasted a year or so
But you ended up with
Some exquisite lingerie

Buttfuck Christ and Chicken Tenders at the Galactical, Fantastical, Truck Stop Found on the Jefferson Parish Trail

Buttfuck Christ and chicken tenders at the
    galactical
Fantastical truck stop found on the Jefferson
Parish trail
Confession
Penance
Circumstance and mystery of misery,
    besides;

Dance, my sweet cuckoldress!

February on the coast is never simple
Last September's hurricane debris is
    sacrament
Unction
At the junction of

Fantasy and fear

The far away and here

Drive-through coffee sacrilege and red lights

Neon echoes bottled

Drank in dank motel rooms, alone

Flash of fleshy thighs beyond the end zones

Only make my cock swell

Within the dancer's cage

Against her present

Control and chastity and counsel

On the road

Alpha Red

She knows how to hurt me
    yet, never harm
How to torment and tease
    when I plead, "Please"
To smile with red lips, empowered, Alpha
    as the welts rise
As tears well in my eyes
She takes and locks away
That hidden little piece of me
 I save for only her to see
As reparations
For all the nights she's had to sleep
    unrequited
As the satisfaction of her lover
Pooled and cooled
And soaked into the sheets
Beneath her
No more

Neither mortal time nor distance

Can deny her

Heat and steel resolve

She holds me firm

Oh, my sacred fuck,

She knows how to hurt me

And never bring me harm

Even in tender moments

When we both lay most exposed

The Queen needn't be reminded

of the power in the flame

That drew me near

The Furs of Venus never scorched as tender

As when she calls to me

Petitioning surrender

In those few dark

And perfectly formed moments

when the storm has barely quelled

When she slowly brings me back
From inner space

Her Alpha lips
Those dark, deep, eyes
Her ecclesiastic face

suck

his clear green eyes darted
side to side as I filled his mouth
thinking of his wife's tight and sweet
cunny of flesh in Premont

IED reflux and border patrol check-point
questions answered with apologies
unspoken
seatbelts fastened and secured
Nebraska's under water this morning
    so I hear

father Franklin Tower I remember
that basement in Roswell
pulling engines off of airliners in the
    daytime
orange glow from Artesia oilfields mark
    horizons
        at night

how do we get there
she always knew exactly when to leave
when drinks would turn to darker things
as reptile passions satiated lust
    and he'd go down before me
        on his knees

Score

That chick that was crashing at Lisa's place
Mexican Lisa, used to live off Central
Before she caught that case
Shows up with two big ass bottles of pills
Never tells me where she got 'em
And I didn't much care
Said we should get right tonight
Said she'd suck my cock

Long tablets, scored once,
Sickly yellow like crusty linoleum
Like chalk
You put three or four in a big spoon, a
     tablespoon
Give them a cold water rinse
Crush and soak the pills
Stir that slush in the spoon
With the little plastic end from the plunger

Use the BD brand, with UltraFine tips
Throw in a little piece torn from a cigarette
    filter
Draw it up into the barrel. You're loaded
If shit's gone right, you end up with a
One mL shot of yellow liquid that looks like
    fresh piss
Knock that fucker into the crook of your arm
    and take a little break
Maybe a nap.

When you wake up, if she's still there.
Start soaking another round of pills.
See if she's still down to suck
Scratch your nose. Find your lighter.
Blaze that cigarette.
Ask that chick that was crashing at Lisa's
    place
If she wants a drag or two
From the one with the torn filter

Someone should probably scrape

The fucking spoon clean

Before we hit that shit

Again

Driving Stoned in North Chicago

I am driving stoned in North Chicago
Waukegan Avenue, all the way to Fountain
    Square
And, I'm hitting every light green, mile after
    mile
Charmed
Blessed
One of those cold April nights, when Winter
    reminds us
She'll stay as long as she pleases

And I'd be jazzed
If things were different
If you hadn't just told me about the biopsies
That came back malignant
Cancer
And it's spread
To the lymph nodes

But, not to tell anyone else, just yet

And, you brew coffee
Strong, boiled, stove top...dangerous
And we smoke in your kitchen
American Spirits from the yellow box,
Then, a joint of some hydro-grown sativa
    strain
We do the math in dog years, 8...maybe 7
Since we last shared space

Before Sacred Wounds set my words to
    wheels

It all flies by
Like driving stoned, at night
And hitting every light green
Red reserved for canvas tennis shoes
And other lanes of traffic
Other avenues
To heaven

International District Morning

Roosters crow
Feathers and comb
Jazzy, funky, cacophonic
Trumpet tunes

They are using runway 2-6 this morning
From the coasts, they're flying in
Frontier A-319's
And Boeing Southwest color schemes
Gear down, engines tear the air
On short final

Winter morning clears customs
And is ushered onto
The International District
Cockle, Lockle, Doodly, Poodly, Doo!

Get up and put the coffee on

Let the dog out

Cold red brick floor

24 degrees

Stoke the fire dregs

Piñón smoke scent occupies the city

Uniting us

In quiet community

Daily mass of solar resurrection

Dreams are left on bedsides

To be forgotten

Light snow glows atop adobe walls

Waiting for

The sun to come

Streaking over Sandia Crest

Tune into the public radio

As the poultry crow

Their feathered salute of centuries

Daily bread, sunny eggs

Cackle, crackle, smackled shells

Tortillas y chile verde,
mixed in Albuquerque morning

Red Tulips

We all know

The reason behind the season

Even

Red tulips

Two, Three days past perfection

Splay their petals

In obscene splendor

Not hiding nor concealing

Any intimacy

In the rapidly

Burning

Daylight

Of Spring

Boogie Fights

Lace up your purse and let's go
Twist and tread to the radio

Mind your boundaries
As you tear down walls

Retrogrades and ascendancies
　　are more than anything else
　　　　matters of perspective
　　　　　and interpretation

This is not the time to stop dancing

Sandhills

Washed out state highways
Through Nebraska sandhills
I have left the cranes and other things
    behind me
In the New Mexico, Apache bosque
At the end of winter
Driving on to Dakota Dignity

Flood waters make their own way
Upon and across the continent
They wash away and undercut concrete
And leave flotsam along the roadways of
    our ever-moving dreams
Racing radial tires spin like mad mandalas
Like mysteries dissolved by FM radio

There will be more rain, yet
Falling upon my road-burned heart

And poetry

And April snow

Before the cranes come home

Before I see my

Desert mountain

Sanctuary

Adobe

Again

When She Kissed Me

When she took my hand
It was like uncured cement
Stuck to the side of the mixer

When she kissed me
It tasted like menthol cigarettes
And a bloody lip

When she went down on me
She gagged like a cliff diver
Swallowing the sea

When she fucked me
(And, damn, did she fuck me)
It felt like drunk galaxies
Dancing to greasy jazz
In a Jackson, Mississippi juke joint

And when she slept next to me
Her breathing sounded like
An air-tight seal, opening and closing

When she tortured me
It was delicious penitence
Like a 12 month parole set-off

And, when she left me

It was like all the secrets in the world
Were being spelled out, in an alphabet
That I would never learn to read

Friday

Celestial bodies and water-bearers
Women in my Solar System
Tell me that they care for me
But
They say
They don't
They can't
Trust themselves around me
For fear of being swept away
By feelings
Lust
Love
And
Losing themselves
Being eclipsed

I live in Walter White's hometown
Fuck it

He's as real

As any, given, part of who I am

I haven't gotten called for a paid gig

In almost a year

No one reads, or buys

The shit I write

I have no heirs, no protégée

No family that matter

My best friend, my old dog

Probably won't be alive, this time, next year

And the inanity and mass-delusion

Of the holidays

The Holy Days

Are queued to disturb the status quo, again

No matter what

I do hate those red letter days

Why not just go and blow
A thousand or so
On street Meth and questionable company
With people that do
Trust themselves around me?

New Year's Day
Would be
A nice, round date to mark
An end of yet another beginning

Fuck it
It's Blues night on the university radio
I'll probably feel better,
Come Friday

You all
Always seem
So fucking
Excited about Friday

Hotel Bars and Black Town Cars

Have you come here tonight
To assist me in perpetuating
The lie
    of the
        successful, traveling, poet?

Hope whispers,
Even as
    experience screams

Hiding from ourselves
Our evil, aimless, selves
In hotel bars and black town cars
On the way to where we're going
Dark glasses on the transit train
Earbuds on the airplane
Pre-packaged podcast validation of our
obvious

And we hold signs that shout
"No Walls!"

How often I wrap myself in the familiar me
Return to cities
That I came to know decades ago
Like comfortable, old, lovers
Flaws embraced, like the weather
Songs that once defined our lives
Worn thread bare by the seasons

A woman next to me
At the airport gate in Oakland
Code switches Chinese and English
Talking into her phone
And, I try
But cannot bring to mind
    the last time
I set out to find
    the unknown

Contradictions and omissions
Circus tents and hunting seasons

So, off she's gone to Florida
I think she just stopped believing the lies of
my life
Mixed with gin and dreams
Little poetry magazines

My hopes whisper
My experience screams

Daughter of Doubt

Dark, dark, daughter of doubt
Cast aside and sent away
To hide the shame that your scars and tears
Pull from the hearts of delicate men
Surrender your burden
On the banks of the Missouri

Arches and spires are liars aflame
But, this is not an era of truth
Tulips bloom in Tower Grove Park, and
    daffodils
As stones are gathered up to seal the tomb
Isolate yourself inside
Aside from the stations of your loss

All those beat beatitudes
Flor de Leurs and used syringes
Cast aside and sent away

To landfills and incinerators
Splendid relics suspended from your
　　doorframe
Our Lady of Horrors entertains and lulls us

Here comes quiet dragon passionless candor

There is nothing here to care about
Just waiting on our phones to charge
Our plans to change
Your time to come
At last, after centuries
Dark, dark, daughter of doubt

Justified in your simplicity, singular in your
duplicity
Designed and cut to fit
The click and paste
Of human waste

It is probably time to dredge the fucking
　　river
And run naked to the sea, away from men
　　like me

From desert motel rooms
In late September
To all the ancient mysteries of lust
And light
And need
And loss

A Road Poet Counts His Blessings

Bless all

The miles I've traded away for poetry

That have ended up as

Slimy condoms tossed without thought into

   corners

Of cut-rate motel rooms

After open mics and features

Package shows and MC events

As fleshy high school

English teachers clean themselves

With scratchy white towels

In over-lit

Under-sized

Water closets

Off highway exits

Before returning to

Salesmen husbands

Until the next time

I return

To upend

Suburban applecart hearts

And status quo circumstance

That have all ended up as

Gregory Corso gigolo cigarette butts

Glowing for a nanosecond in the slipstream

    from my window

85 mph at night onto the bi-wayside

Beneath the desert Milky Way

200 miles from anywhere that matters

The miles I have traded for poetry

The years I'll never get back

I would have wasted them, anyway

Dead Cohen and I are drinking tonight, and
Driving
West, always west
From Christ's cunt-like ever-empty grail

In Poetica Sanguinis, Ipso
Amen

The Death of the Straight, White, Malepoet

Death is not erasure
Only the grossest and most undeniable,
   the things that most claim to
      love the most or hate,
End
The rest is indelible
The stains, like red wine
Blood of blonde-haired Christ
On Christmas Eve eternal
The sacramental stains remain
To chase their own distortions
Through the decades...even into centuries

Let us all, now, consider
The death of the Straight, White, Malepoet

Is my eulogy premature?

Is this mourning out of time?

Out of place?

Should we mourn at all?

Can we?

Let us now sing a dirge

For the death of the love poem

Penned in pining for the fair-haired vestal
 virgin feminine, unrequited

The death of hometown homage celebrating
 water-tower towns and pickup trucks

And hunting wildlife with the patriarchs,
 every autumn

The death of meat-fisted examinations and
 projections upon the other

The uncivilized, the unchurched, the savage

The deviation from the norm, the pervert

The norm that was

The Straight, White, Malepoets' to define

Bringing to the indigenous, unasked for

Death

Killing

Rape and armed evangelism

Slavery and legal systems

Could not displace, replace, nor erase

What was here

Before they waxed poetic and claimed

The world new, and theirs, and in need of

    gunpoint salvation

And took it all

How the Straight, White, Malepoets

Categorized and cat-called

How they and they alone decided what

Real poetry was

What about hip hop, street pops

What about the Sun Dances and magic Sufi

nights

Jazz and Rock and Roll must be the Devil's
    music
To the Straight, White, Malepoets
It was
The beginning of the end

So, double down on Shakespeare
And stop by woods on snowy evenings
Guaranteed to be seen in the syllabus

The death of the Straight, White, Malepoet
    is upon us
Just as he has feared for years
His death was told in Roma tea leaves
By the pyramids of Yucatan, in Pueblo kivas

His death was certain and eventual when
Coltrane blew Supreme
Like Gabriel the arch-angel in Harlem

When Kaufman and queer Allen beat
beatitudes in wonder

Attitude
Groove
Beats and bops and funk and blues
And Maya's caged bird singing
Like Gorman church bells ringing
The call to prayer is sounded
Holy requiem

The stains remain to be reclaimed
As collected and classic volumes of denial
It's being too damned self-satisfied by the
    words sung
In Negro spirituals
To hear or feel the pain, the pride
The poetry that needs no Moses
To lead no one, nowhere, no how, man
The poetry was always there!

The death of the Straight, White, Malepoet
Is a fact, at long last
It is not the death of poetry!
The pages and the brains they stained
    remain

We're gonna need darker ink to tell this
    truth from here on out
Coming out in a million different shades of
    rainbow wandering
From alleys, singing freedom songs,
    rejoicing
Into midnights lit by neon leather drag kings

Burroughs blowjobs on the border
The invisible ink of centuries is over
And he no longer gets to decide
What is and isn't poetry

The Straight, White, Malepoet's gatekeeping

Keys have rusted and the gate itself is
    creaking
Tired of the shame and shushing
Hideous hinges, too staid to swing
For any but the dead, themselves

Buried in their libraries and classroom
    mausoleums
Let us gather here and everywhere
Not to honor, but to bury
To end, but not erase

We pace the cage he placed us in
Like raulsalinas and Etheridge Knight and
    Baca
I apologize for the apologetics and the
Apostasy within me
But I cannot stay in my lane
This is a motherfucking intersection!
And it always should be

We will not rot and gather dust upon his
    shelves
I will not politely raise my hand and wait my
    turn
Let the Straight, White, Malepoet
Burn in effigy to ash
He knows his time has passed
It's been eons in the making

Let every immigrant song alive rise up
And scream above the silence
Speak glory through the violence
Ring like freedom's 'sposed to ring

Women own the means of publicity and
    production
And reproduction on the page
The day is here
We're queer
    and our poems will take the day
        away

From the dead and the dying
The covetous and the lying

Let's crash his wake with slams and
Instagram
And ganja dagga saxophones and kimchi
    covered couplets
Right out loud

Those credentials will look great upon your
    tombstone,
You Straight, White, Malepoet
You're dead, I say,
Now die already

We'll always have your stains
They'll never wash away.

The Sky is a Different Thing

The mountain stands so strong and true, it
    will never be fully tamed
As men pass through and ages pass, each
    lends it a different name
Mysteries and mystics, full of fantasies and
    prayers
Children play around its base in crisp, green,
    forest air
Necessity and virtue pass like eagles on the
    wind
Stars will rise and snow will melt,
The seasons 'round in ring
That mountain stands firm and fast-

The sky is a different thing

Our ocean deep and tranquil, safe; or
    choppy over shoals

Unknown treasures hidden deep, and
    creatures yet unknown
When you chase horizons blue and bold, it'll
    float you home again
Wheel and rudder guide your way on
    moon-tide sailor tunes
Coral reefs and harbor towns, sea view misty
    dreams
The final peace of drowning men on
    albatrosses' wing
Our ocean currents navigate-

The sky is a different thing

The sky is a different thing
It's bigger than your dreams
The sky envelops everything
    on hoof, with scales, or wings
And gravity, oh, gravity
    it always ends the same

Let earthquakes destroy your shores-

The sky is a different thing

To wake up high, above the clouds-
    with heaven just above
Ants and armies toil below, for faith and
    rage and love
Vapor trails, the Milky Way, stars on autumn
    nights
Holy women burning sage, exhale magic
    from their pipe
Content to be conditional, like pigeons
    eating clay

Melt the phone books, dial tones
    It's going to be okay

Tears of joy flow down your cheeks, on knee
with golden ring

For time and all eternity-

The sky is a different thing

Fall

Forsake me, lover; and all my sins
You know that I must be leaving again
Like that country song we used to sing,
The highway never ends

I bury sunflower seeds in the summer
And mums sprout back every spring
When the Monarchs come through and the
    temperature drops
I'll have blooms in my garden, again

Red mountain finches and white wing doves
C-130's and perennial loves
Head south for the season, and lives fly by
And, I'm aching, seeking a way to stay high

Most of the poets give birth in the spring
    time

With hope and recollection

Tomato cages and high desert rain
I finally stopped chasing hurricanes
I'll harvest my thoughts and catch up on my
    prayers
When sunny morning chill fills the autumnal
    air

Welcome Mat

I need to replace the welcome mat
Inside the gate
Of my casita's adobe-walled courtyard

It's been worn with the weight
Of three winters
Of many writer visitors

Friends and lovers and
I suppose there is a poem
Here somewhere

But, I am fresh out of
All that Red Wheelbarrow transcendence
And all of those everyday insights

So, I am off to the
Discount chain department store

To buy a new one

As soon as

I find

My keys

Red Sugar Water

Late March and
I am not moving much this Spring
No one is

I saw the first hummingbird of this year's
    migration
Flitting about my garden today

A famished, frantic, twiggy little
Emerald-throated fellow

Suspended there
Like the next guy they crucified
After the crowd cleared at Golgotha
The weekend after Easter

Just hanging there, skinny and withering
With messages fresh from the Copper
    Canyon

And, it makes me feel vital

Necessary

Essential

Christ-ish

When I fill the sugar-water feeder

At 23 Thousand

The death count was 23 thousand in my
    nation
As I stood in my kitchen
Screen door open
Holding my warm coffee cup
And smoking
Watching large, fluffy, quarantine snowflakes
    glide
Onto petite tulip blooms

In April
Like that melancholy song of mourning
By Prince

Long past any chance of avoiding anything
We're all along for the ride
Mostly asleep in the backseat
No one behind the wheel

Microbes and facemasks

Facebook and poets reading poems to
    themselves

In the digital Universe

Hoping our voices

Would not be forgotten

Among the thousands

Rye Seed

For the 2nd day in a row
I find myself incredibly mentally altered
Not disturbed
Before noon
I know this because
At some point I recognize the Native
American
Call in talk show
On the public radio, inside
And that show ends at noon, on weekdays

If the worst thing they can say
About me, when this is over,
Is that I spent most of it
Sitting stoned alone
In my garden
Feeding mountain finches
Rye seed from my faded red feeder

Then,

That's exactly what they can say...

The Cadence of Revelation

The cadence of revelation is echoing
From DNA to Do Not Disturb
    as clear as destiny
And we ascend the crystalline totem without
    filter

We scanned the heavens and horizon
We struggled to stand in the fulfilled grace
of agony
    and plundered the last behest of the
      ancients
With a daub of design forced upon the
    tragedy,
The day I stumbled stoned into oblivion

A fool surge in timing
This high tide of chance will prevail
Where confusion and delusion thrive

The rasp of dry cough cacophony
    trying to venture beyond
Coming to heel

Marked and marred by the daily trauma of
    trust

Irrational Numbers

When did you stop following the numbers?
When did it all become one ignored thing
    to you?

After 5 thousand?
After 10?
Did it even matter, to you, past 100,000?
200? A quarter million? A half?

The popular mathematics of carnage
One life's value amid the millions
That Spring counted its own time
Without rhyme

Greater than
Less than
Division and disenfranchisement
Exponential loss

There are no more rational numbers

Nikolai Medtner's Blues

Dark and violent classical piano

Plays on the dollar store, solid state,

Off-brand, radio

Minor tones with syncopation

Sonata Tragica

As she packs up all her

Clothes and cosmetics

And is sure to grab

My last pack of smokes

On her way out the door

I'm still waiting for my summons from Lhasa

A letter from my Maharaja

I'm waiting in line to clear customs

Declaring everything, seen and unseen

Known and unknown

Forcing down the afterbirth of revolt

And smoking sativa in my sunflower garden

Wearing masks in public
Socially whistling past the graveyard

Sometimes

Sometimes I try to bargain
    with the tiny, flying, insects in my
        garden

"Dude," I say,
"I don't mind if you wanna
Tickle walk, creep and crawl
    around on my leg...you can do that
All day,
Just don't bite me, okay?"

And,
Sometimes I just reach for the swatter,
And cuss at myself
    if I miss

Buying Cigarettes on Sunday on Central Avenue

It was Sunday.
The day
We all seek out, or conspicuously avoid
Our idols
Our virtues
Check in with
Whoever, Whatever
We think, we hope, we dream, we feel
Is keeping score

Mine, that morning, was nicotine.
I'd smoked my last, from my last pack, with
my first cup of morning coffee.
So, there I was. It was close to noon on
Central Avenue. Top down, bulldog riding
shotgun, past the casino and racetrack, past
the weekend fairground flea market, car

washes, pawn shops, and motor hotels. Past
the shopping carts filled with everything
some folks can claim as their own.
We were headed to that smoke shop; the
one next to that store-front Christian street
mission on the edge of Nob Hill.

Cash transaction
2 packs, 15 fucking dollars
I've always been willing
to pay for my vices
Upfront, and out of pocket
when required

Lighting up, parked on the curb of some
side-street. Yesss...
Almost as good as the first time. almost as
thrilling as original sin, naked in the garden.
Almost fucking perfect, and undeniably
fleeting.

My dog, beside me, looked to me with the eyes of a temple custodian.

Back out on Central, we turn our backs to the brunches and hip, vintage, retail. We pass families out on foot, carrying back simple treasures from the flea market, just like Leslie and I carried back that vase and that iron candelabra that we found there, right after we moved here, a neighborhood rich with new immigrants.

A striking, ebony skinned, woman, wrapped in vibrant African textile is walking, a block or two east of Louisiana. Her hand was cupped upon her daughter's shoulder, in front of her.

10, 11 years old.

And the child is grasping one of those large, plastic, dress-up dolls; the ones that run about 3 feet tall or so. She's got her dark arms wrapped around that doll in a way that

tells the

Entire

Holy

Universe

that...

THIS

IS

MINE

The stringy, blonde, pseudo-hair is not
nearly as jarring to me as the layers of
contrast broadcast, set off by, the faded,
peach plastic, nudity of stark, white, breast
buds and chubby, baby-fat, thighs stretched
by commerce and design for toy-aisle
voyeurs.

And, of course all the cultural and social analogies hit me like deep indica. They roil in my mind.

Black and white
Not abstract
Image and reality
How it looks and how it feels

That toothy smile, and that proud, guiding, hand. On a Sunday, a new week, in a new world. For that girl, who was still a girl, but wouldn't be one forever, it looked like it felt divine.
Like knowing that there is something you can hold on to, even as you know something's holding you.

Not even the first smoke from a fresh pack on a mild, May, morning can beat that

Acknowledgements

Some of the poems were first published by

Under the Bleachers

The Dope Fiend Daily

Otherwise Engaged

Dream Noir Arts Journal

Boundless 2018

Central Coast Poetry Shows

Culture Cult Magazine

Synchronized Chaos

Mad Swirl

Boundless 2019

The Local Train Magazine

Houston Poetry Fest 2019

Windward Review

Otherwise Engaged

North Beach and Other Stories, Hercules
Publishing

Anacua Lit Arts Journal

Thanks and appreciation to the Rio Grande
Valley International Poetry Festival, Kaktus
Brewing reading series, Wordspace, Stone
Spiral Coffee, The Houston Poetry Festival,
Full Circle Book Co-op, The Beat Museum,
Hasta Muerte Coffee, and everyone that has
come out to join us on the road.

Biography

PW Covington has spent decades crisscrossing the American continent, collecting and sharing poetry.

Both his poetry and short fiction have been nominated for the Pushcart Prize, and he has been invited to perform from The Beat Museum in San Francisco to the Havana International Poetry Festival in Cuba.

A service-connected disabled veteran and convicted felon, Covington's work stems from lived experience and an understanding of the Universal natures of sin and struggle, across cultural and geographic frontiers. Find his message in jail cells, down alleys, in smoke-filled back rooms, and out on the highway...always the highway.

Covington has published a novel, edited Indie literary journals, and collaborated with other writers and artists on a variety of socially engaged projects. This is his 5th collection of poetry.

Find and follow him on social media for updates about readings, performances, and current projects.

Other Volumes from Gnashing Teeth Publishing

Heat the Grease, We're Frying Up Some Poetry anthology

Love Notes You'll Never Read anthology

Winter limited release zine

Rain Minnows [Notecards and Poems] by Joshua Bridgwater Hamilton

Insurrection anthology

Forthcoming Books

SHE: Seen. Heard. Engaged. youth anthology

Meditations & Mediations by Dr. Rebecah Hall

Places I never want to see again (they remind me of you who I once loved) by Keriann Gilson

You can purchase our books at
http://gnashingteethpublishing.com

Made in the USA
Middletown, DE
28 April 2021